JANIS JOPLIN

THE QUEEN OF PSYCHEDELIC ROCK

Simon Braund

Foreword by
Joel Selvin

Publisher's Note: Readers will note that the sharpness of the images in this book varies. This is to be expected of photography from this era and of this nature. Images have been chosen not just for their quality, but also for their intimacy and evocative insight into Janis Joplin's history.

Publisher and Creative Director: Nick Wells

Commissioning Editor: Polly Prior

Art Director: Mike Spender

Layout Design: Jane Ashley

Digital Design & Production: Chris Herbert

Special thanks to: Karen Fitzpatrick, Dawn Laker, Catherine Taylor and Jen Veall

FLAME TREE PUBLISHING

6 Melbray Mews, Fulham,

London SW6 3NS, United Kingdom

www.flametreepublishing.com

First published 2020

20 22 24 23 21

1 3 5 7 9 10 8 6 4 2

© 2020 Flame Tree Publishing Ltd

ISBN: 978-1-83964-229-6

A CIP record for this book is available from the British Library.

Printed in China | Created, Developed & Produced in the United Kingdom

JANIS JOPLIN

THE QUEEN OF PSYCHEDELIC ROCK

Simon Braund

Foreword by
Joel Selvin

FLAME TREE
PUBLISHING

Contents

Foreword

Was there ever an entertainer who wanted to be loved by her audience more than Janis Joplin? That desperate need filled every breath she took onstage, which, in part, accounted for the extraordinary intensity of her performances. That was no act; that was her life. Her biography followed her – the lonely little girl who couldn't find love, looking for it in applause – and when Janis Joplin sang the blues, her whole life flashed before everyone's eyes.

She was San Francisco's first hippie queen, the 'chick singer' with Big Brother and the Holding Company, one of the five bands who started the psychedelic ballroom scene. Her pin-up poster sold in Haight Ashbury head shops before the band even made a record. She had finally found a place in life where she belonged and was not merely accepted but celebrated – the exact opposite of her life growing up in Texas.

She was a comet that blazed across the skies of the Woodstock generation, blasting out of the underground with a boozy drawl and a ragged voice that could wrench the pain and anguish out of a song like nobody since Billie Holiday. Despite all the bravado, bonhomie and barnyard epithets, she could never fully disguise the hurt little girl underneath and it was exactly that vulnerability that brought her songs to life.

The pain eventually became too much for her to handle and the tragic end may have been inevitable but in a few short years, she left behind a mark that time will never erase.

Joel Selvin

Why Janis?

The news of Janis Joplin's death from a heroin overdose, alone in a Hollywood motel room on 4 October 1970, shocked the world. It was the knockout punch of a vicious double whammy. Just 16 days earlier, Jimi Hendrix had died in London from a lethal cocktail of booze and pills. The music world had lost two of its towering figures in as many weeks.

An Exclusive Group

Hendrix and Joplin were both three years shy of their 30th birthdays when they died. Alongside The Rolling Stones' Brian Jones, who had drowned in his swimming pool earlier that year, they were the founder members of the morbidly named 27 Club, that exclusive group of celebrities whose lives were snuffed out at the same tragically young age. Barely six months later, they were joined by Jim Morrison, lead singer of The Doors, and more recently by Kurt Cobain and Amy Winehouse, a very different singer from Joplin stylistically, but one of few who could match her for heart-rending intensity.

'Maybe I won't last as long as other singers, but I think you can destroy your now by worrying about tomorrow.'

JANIS JOPLIN

Essence Of The Blues

Born in Texas in 1943, Janis began her career as a folk singer, tagging on to the tail end of the beatnik era before finding her true vocation in the blues. Her heroes were Lead Belly, Big Mamma Thornton and Bessie Smith. Her talent was not that she sang like them, but that she sang like herself, tapping into the primal essence of the blues in a way that no other white artist had done before.

'I just opened my mouth and that's what I sounded like.'

JANIS JOPLIN

In The Spotlight

Joplin's first taste of fame came in 1966 as lead singer with psychedelic rock band Big Brother and the Holding Company, then amassing a strong following on the San Francisco scene. According to some accounts, she spent most of her first gig with

JJ, c. 1970

'There's no patent on soul.'

JANIS JOPLIN

Big Brother seated on an amp, waggling a tambourine while they blew minds with some protracted, free-form improvisations. That didn't last long. Joplin's searingly powerful voice and magnetic stage presence soon put her firmly in the spotlight.

Hell-For-Leather

Her rise to stardom came amid the momentous changes sweeping America in the late 1960s – the so-called counterculture – an explosion of new music, fashion and radical

Sam Houston Stadium, November 1969

'She had the unique ability to really tap into her pain and to project it.'

CHET HELMS

thinking that rippled out from its epicentre in the Haight-Ashbury district of San Francisco. As much for her flamboyant look, and hell-for-leather lifestyle, as her vocal talent, Joplin became a leading light of the movement, the living embodiment of the free-love hippie ethos. To those who breathed the heady air of the Haight, she was a goddess; to those who did not, she was a spaced-out, sexually promiscuous menace. That, of course, only added to her appeal; a fascination she still holds half a century after her death.

Joplin had the courage to be a real rebel, to live life on her own terms at a time when only a third of American women went out to work. Those terms, however, were unforgiving. In her four short years at the top, she changed the face of popular music and set the stage for every female rock singer who followed her. What she could not do was conquer the addictive side of her huge personality, and for that she paid the ultimate price.

Something About The Girl

When Janis Joplin sings, purring, bawling, pleading, her eyes screwed shut, every sinew of her body straining to wring the last agonized drop of emotion from a lyric – a single word, even – you have to wonder what fathomless well of bad luck and broken dreams she's drawing from. Her idol was Bessie Smith, and like Smith she must surely have been born into heartache, a hardscrabble childhood, poverty, sorrow and loss, the stuff of the blues. Where else could that voice have come from?

Small-Town Oddball

It came, in fact, not from some backwater bayou or inner-city ghetto but from suburban Texas, nurtured by a middle-class family whose approval she continued to seek and to value even at the peak of her fame. She was a misfit in high school, and suffered the consequences – taunting, name-calling and ostracization, the gamut of small-minded teenage malice – but she had the sweetest revenge: success, and she relished it. The deepest scars her adolescence left her with were from

Fillmore East, New York, March 1968

recurring bouts of acne. So how did a small-town oddball, spotty, overweight and shunned by the cool kids, become the incarnation of free-spirited, tortured-soul decadence, an electrifying emblem of her generation, the hippie-chick pinup who could, in the words of music journalist Richard Goldstein, 'Sing the chic off any listener'?

JJ, c. 1970

Nagging Muse

One answer to that is sheer commitment and single-minded determination to succeed. Even though she knew, deep down, that following her star to become a singer would be her doom, there was no other road open to her. When her first foray into the San Francisco scene came to nothing, it was as much the fear that she was failing, as it was her descent into drug addiction, that brought her back to Texas. But her need outpaced her fears and before long, her nagging muse had lured her away again. And this time, aside from one unhappy school reunion, there was no looking back..

'Nobody has come close to capturing the way that that girl sang ... there is something in her voice that can't be replicated.'

ALICE ECHOLS, BIOGRAPHER

'Joplin [made songs] her own in a way few singers dare to do. She did not sing them so much as struggle with them, assault them'

ELLEN WILLIS, ROCK'N'ROLL WRITER

JJ, c. 1968

The Voice

Of course, all the commitment in the world would have meant nothing if she hadn't also been supremely gifted. Her voice was ferociously raw, untainted by formal training and all the better for it. In 1968, even rattling around in the cavernous void of a D.C. ice skating rink, it moved opera critic John Segraves, of the *Washington Evening Star*, to write: 'Her vocal talents are boundless ... In a proper room, I would imagine there would be no adjectives to describe her.'

Actually, there are many, but they are quickly exhausted. Allied to her titanic charisma, the emotional force of Janis's voice had the power to render listeners all but speechless.

There's a moment in D.A. Pennebaker's documentary film of the 1967 Monterey Pop festival where the camera cuts away from Joplin to pick out Cass Elliot of The Mammas and the Papas seated in the crowd, her gaze riveted to the stage. Later, while Joplin and her band, Big Brother and the Holding Company, bask in tumultuous applause, a clearly awestruck Elliot turns to her companion and mouths two words: 'Oh, wow!'. Which is it, in a nutshell.

'You got to get it while you can.'

JANIS JOPLIN

1942-61: Little Girl Blue

Port Arthur, Texas, is an unprepossessing oil town on the banks of the Sabine Lake, a few miles north of the Gulf of Mexico. It is humid as hell and steeped in the Cajun traditions of neighbouring Louisiana.

'They don't treat beatniks too good in Texas. [They] thought I was a beatnik, though they'd never seen one and neither had I.'

JANIS JOPLIN

Port Arthur, 1958

Fellow Arthurians

It is also the hometown of avant-garde artist Robert Rauschenberg, and one Jiles Perry Richardson Jr, better known as The Big Bopper, portly rockabilly crooner famed for both his 1958 hit 'Chantilly Lace' and for perishing in the same plane crash as Richie Valens and Buddy Holly. The Bopper staked his claim on immortality at the age of 28. Janis Joplin, the city's most notorious native, beat him by a year, dying at the age of 27.

Bohemian Airs

Janis Lyn Joplin was born in Port Arthur on 19 January 1943. Her mother, Dorothy, was a business college registrar; her father, Seth, was an engineer at the Texaco refinery. She had a younger brother, Michael, and a younger sister, Laura. Janice's family were the proverbial church-going pillars of the community, relatively

'Texas is OK if you want to settle down and do your own thing quietly, but it's not for outrageous people, and I was always outrageous.'

JANIS JOPLIN

'I never seemed to be able to control my feelings, to keep them down.'

JANIS JOPLIN

open-minded by the standards of the region. When Janis began to exhibit artistic leanings, they encouraged her, affording her special attention over her sister and brother. She later claimed she fought with her mother, but their clashes seem to have been no more rancorous than between any other rebellious teen and their parents. On the whole, her early upbringing was remarkably conventional.

She began singing in high school, where she fell in with a crowd of blues aficionados. Listening to their records, she was transported by the music of Lead Belly, Ma Rainey and Bessie Smith. In the mournful strains of these scratchy 78s, the seeds of her future were sown. But for now, her Bohemian airs did not sit well with the rest of the Thomas Jefferson High student body. She was branded a 'freak', a 'creep' and, inevitably, a 'nigger-lover'. 'I was a misfit,' she admitted. 'I read, I painted, I thought. I didn't hate niggers.'

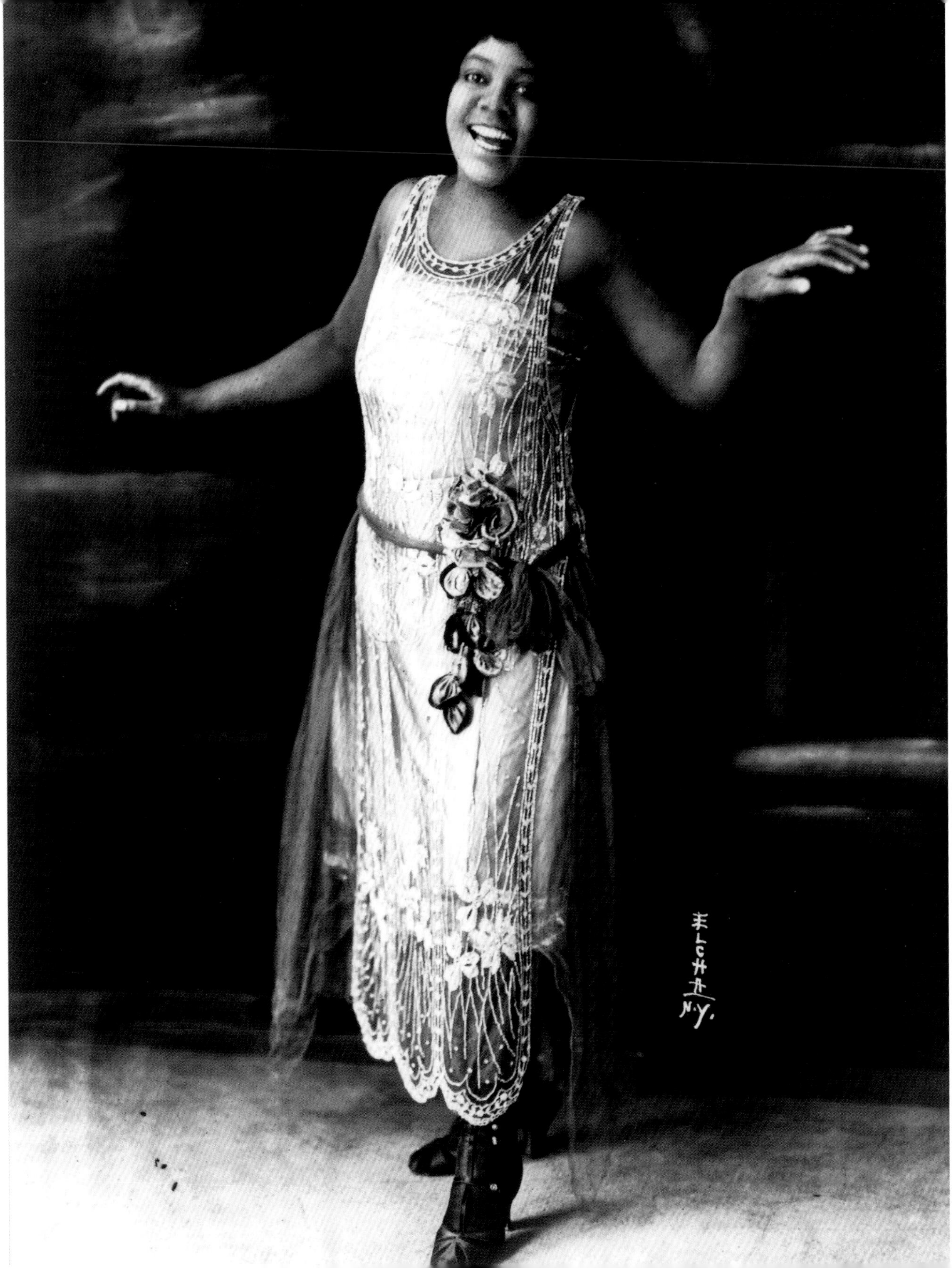

Bessie Smith, c. 1923

'[My classmates] laughed me out of class, out of town, out of the state.'

JANIS JOPLIN

California Dreaming

In 1960, Joplin enrolled at the University of Texas, Austin, where her nonconformist ways created a far more positive stir. A profile in the student paper said: '[She] wears Levi's to class because they're more comfortable, and carries her Autoharp with her everywhere she goes so that in case she gets the urge to break into song, it will be handy. Her name is Janis Joplin.' A persona was emerging.

Joplin began spending time in California in the summer of 1960, hanging out with the local beatniks in Venice. Austin bar owner Ken Threadgill recalled first seeing her in 1961. 'She was just a kid,' he said. 'She worked part-time as a keypunch operator to help pay expenses. She was around off and on from '61 to '63.' Threadgill claimed she showed up at his bar after receiving hospital treatment in San Francisco for drug use. At one of her first performances at Threadgill's, Janis won two bottles of Lone Star beer. In another, she

Beatnik coffee house, Venice, California

'Who you are is
what you settle for,
you know?'

JANIS JOPLIN

Odetta, 1956

and her band won $10 in a talent competition. Threadgill said: 'Actually, she didn't go over so well around here. She was singing in a high, shrill bluegrass kind of sound.' That changed one night at a party in Port Arthur when an impersonation of singer and civil rights activist Odetta produced results that surprised even her. From that point on, Janis had the blues.

Texas Farewell

In January 1962, she began singing at the Purple Onion in Houston and recorded a jingle, 'This Bank Is Your Bank', for a bank in Nacogdoches. She began to attract attention with local bluegrass band the Waller Creek Boys, singing numbers by Lead Belly, Rosie Maddox and Bessie Smith. Away from the stage, though, things were getting complicated. She was dealing weed on campus, experimenting with peyote and taking mammoth doses of barbiturates. When an old friend, Chet Helms, returned from San Francisco with tales of the city's flourishing post-Beat scene, she was all ears. In 1963, she bid a not-so-fond farewell to Texas and decamped to the Bay Area with Helms. Now a budding promoter and manager, his influence on her life would be profound.

1962-65: Try A Little Bit Harder

I f Ken Threadgill is to be believed, Joplin's problems with drugs began early. Even if she wasn't a heavy user when she arrived in San Francisco in 1963, she soon was, developing a taste for speed, flirting with heroin and taking her lifelong love affair with Southern Comfort to a new level. She also got more serious about her music.

Meeting Jorma

At some time in 1963, Joplin met future Jefferson Airplane guitarist Jorma Kaukonen at a folk club in San Jose, California. 'She didn't have a guitar, so she couldn't accompany herself,' recalls Kaukonen. 'We got to talking and she said, "Would you like to back me?" I said I'd be thrilled. I'd never heard anybody sing like that in my life. Even in that moment, I realized I was in the presence of someone very special.'

Jorma Kaukonen, 1967

Kaukonen continued to back Joplin on and off whenever she performed in the Bay Area, and in 1964, they recorded a number of blues standards together on a Monotape machine Kaukonen had bought with money saved from teaching guitar. Kaukonen says, 'We were going over some songs, rehearsing for something, and I just let the tape recorder run – Janis and I are playing music, and my wife at the time is writing a letter in the background. We didn't think about it being special in any way. I just had a tape recorder, so I recorded the stuff I did.'

'Her voice as a blues singer to me was so pure and elegant.'

JORMA KAUKONEN

The Typewriter Tape

The so-called 'Typewriter Tape' was released as a bootleg album decades later. Endearingly lo-fi, and featuring Kaukonen's superb acoustic finger-picking – plus his then-

Telegraph Hill, San Francisco, 1963

JJ. c. 1965

wife Margarita's equally nimble fingers on the typewriter – the recordings are a fascinating snapshot of Joplin at a crossroads in her career. The autoharp folk sound is gone, and her voice has the authentic blues ache, but her trademark roar would come later.

'All you really have that really matters are feelings. That's what music is to me.'

JANIS JOPLIN

Going Nowhere

Kaukonen claims he had no knowledge of Joplin's drug use. On the tape, the between-song banter is relaxed and carefree, she laughs easily. In reality, her life was unravelling. In 1963, she was severely beaten in a street brawl and arrested for shoplifting. By May of 1965, convinced her career was going

nowhere, she was injecting methamphetamine and weighed a skeletal 6 st 2 lb (88 lb). Her friends became so alarmed at her deterioration that they threw a party for her to raise money for a bus ticket back to Texas. Too frail to put up a fight, Joplin went willingly.

Buttoned-Down Bourgeois

Living with her parents again, it seemed her rebel days were over. She traded the beatnik lifestyle, the drugs and the booze for a beehive hairdo and an anthropology major at Lamar University in Beaumont, Texas. In late 1965, she got engaged to an IBM technician named Peter de Blanc, who

'I want to want the white house with the picket fence covered with climbing roses, but I don't.'

JANIS JOPLIN

she first met in San Francisco. As if to emphasize just how buttoned-down bourgeois her world had become, de Blanc travelled from New York to Port Arthur to ask for Janis's hand in marriage.

Joplin also began regular sessions with a psychiatrist. Still haunted by how quickly and decisively drugs had taken hold of her, she was convinced that following her dream to be a singer would mean a relapse into abuse and addiction. The alternative, though, was hardly less harrowing: a return to her job as a keypunch operator, or work as a secretary, settling down and becoming like every other frumpy housewife in Port Arthur. For Janis, there was never really a choice.

Statement Of Intent

Around the same time, Joplin went into the studio to record a handful of songs, among them the original version of her own composition 'Turtle Blues' and, ironically, a cover of Buffy Sainte-Marie's pioneering anti-drug song 'Cod'ine'. Whether this was a statement of intent or not, it's clear that Joplin would not go quietly into suburban domesticity. Even before the recording sessions began, de Blanc had broken off their engagement.

JJ, 1967

'If anyone I knew was destined for stardom, it was Janis. Hands down, no questions about it.'

JORMA KAUKONEN

1965-66: Big Brother

I n 1966, Chet Helms was running a rehearsal space for musicians in the Haight-Ashbury district of San Francisco. A key figure in the Haight's role as nerve centre of the counterculture, Helms was also managing an experimental rock band named Big Brother and the Holding Company. Thanks to regular gigs at the city's Avalon Ballroom, promoted by Helms, Big Brother was attracting a strong local following, and found themselves in the market for a lead singer …

Pure Janis

'I think maybe one or two people in the group were thinking of Signe and the Airplane and how that worked out,' said Big Brother guitarist Sam Andrew in 1970 (Signe Toly Anderson preceded Grace Slick as lead singer for Jefferson Airplane). 'But most of us were thinking of just any vocalist who came along who was good.' Chet said, 'I know this great chick.' Helms duly

Chet Helms, 1967

Janis Joplin and Big Brother and the Holding Company, c. 1967

dispatched his friend Travis Rivers to Texas with instructions to lure Janis back to San Francisco. At the time, Joplin was on the brink of joining Austin-based psychedelic rock pioneers The 13th Floor Elevators, but Rivers got to her first.

Joplin maintained that she resisted returning to San Francisco and only did so because Rivers was good in bed. As she put it to *Rolling Stone* editor David Dalton, 'I was fucked into being in Big Brother.' It's pure Janis, but almost certainly untrue – whatever Rivers' skills in the sack. The idea of resuming her old drug habit still terrified her, but her ambition to succeed won. She agreed to go, even though she'd never sung rock'n'roll before.

'I won't quit to become someone's old lady.'

JANIS JOPLIN

Sing Loud And Move Wild

Joplin's audition with Big Brother was not, apparently, on fire like legend demands. 'We were the established rock and roll band,' recalled Sam Andrew. 'We are doing this woman a favour to even let her come and sing with us … She didn't look like a hippie, she looked like my mother. I mean, she was good, but she had to learn how to do that.'

Janis herself remembered things differently: 'I just exploded,' she said. 'I'd never sung like that before. I sang simple, but you *can't* sing like that in front of a rock and roll band. You *have* to sing loud and move wild. It happened the first time…' Wherever the truth lies, there's no doubt that once Joplin signed on, she had a major impact on Big Brother, their sound shifting from spaced-out improvisations to more orthodox blues-rock to accommodate her. This might have alienated some fans, but with Joplin at centre stage, a whole lot more were waiting in the wings.

'Music's for grooving man, and music's not for puttin' yourself through bad changes, y'know?'

JANIS JOPLIN

With Big Brother and the Holding Company, Avalon Ballroom, 1967

40

Finding Her Groove

Janis made her debut with Big Brother at the Avalon Ballroom on 10 June 1966. By now, the hippie movement in San Francisco was getting into its drug-fuelled groove, with Haight-Ashbury as its epicentre and opposition to the Vietnam War its life force. As house band at the Avalon, Big Brother joined Jefferson Airplane and the Grateful Dead at the forefront of the scene. Janis, her singing voice now at full throttle, and her stage presence growing by the minute, was fast becoming a figurehead in her own right. She did not look like someone's mother any more.

'But when I sing, I feel, oh I feel, well, like when you're first in love.' JANIS JOPLIN

For the time being at least, her personal life was on a relatively even keel. She lived with Rivers for a while (he claimed later she turned down his proposal of marriage), and later moved into a commune of sorts with the band and various partners in Lagunitas, California. Most importantly, she was drug free.

Avalon Ballroom, San Francisco, 1967

'She didn't look like a hippie, she looked like my mother.'

SAM ANDREW

Haight Street, 1967

Missed Opportunity

Thanks largely to Joplin, Big Brother's fortunes continued to rise, especially on the local live circuit. Their first foray into the studio, however, was something of a disaster. After a series of gigs in Chicago, the band were stranded in the city when the promoter refused to pay them enough for their air fare back to California; by this time, they had parted ways with Chet Helms, and were yet to appoint Julius Karpen as their new manager.

Given the circumstances, it's understandable that an offer to sign with local indie label Mainstream Records seemed attractive. In fact, it was a huge mistake. The label, founded by New Yorker Bob Shad in 1964, specialized in Dixieland jazz reissues and had no experience with rock'n'roll at all. Not surprisingly, the recordings completely failed to capture the Big Brother sound. And Shad, too, refused to pay them an advance. 'We asked him for a thousand dollars,' said Sam Andrew. 'He said no. We said five hundred? He said no. Well, can we have the plane fare home? He said not one penny.' According to Andrew, Shad was true to his word; the band never saw a penny from *Big Brother and the Holding Company*, their debut album. It was a missed opportunity, and a bad record that wouldn't see the light of day for another year. It must have been a crushing disappointment, but back in San Francisco, greater things were on the horizon.

1966-67: Having a Ball

Big Brother gigged regularly throughout the latter half of 1966 and into 1967, mostly in smaller venues but occasionally on significantly larger stages – the Hells Angels Wail Party in Panhandle Park, and the first Human Be-In in Golden Gate Park, for instance. Another major event was the Mantra-Rock Dance held at the Avalon Ballroom on 29 January 1967, a fundraiser for the San Francisco Hare Krishna temple.

The Spiritual Equinox

The line-up at the Mantra-Rock Dance boasted Big Brother, Moby Grape, beat poet Allen Ginsberg, the Grateful Dead and Hare Krishna founder, Bhaktivedanta Swami, surely the apotheosis of the hippie ideal. In fact, that would come several months later.

The Monterey Pop Festival took place on 16–18 June 1967 at the Monterey County Fairground in Monterey, California. A ground-

JJ, 1967

breaking assembly of musicians from around the world, including Indian sitar master Ravi Shankar and South African jazz trumpeter Hugh Masekela, it marked the spiritual equinox of the Summer of Love. Preserved for posterity by documentary filmmaker D.A. Pennebaker, it also immortalized the moment that Janis Joplin became not merely a star, but an icon of her generation.

'...when she left the stage I knew that a little bit of my destiny had changed.'

STEVIE NICKS, FLEETWOOD MAC

Blissed Out

Big Brother were originally scheduled to play one set on the Saturday afternoon, sharing the limelight with Canned Heat, the Steve Miller Band, and Country Joe and the Fish. The band were furious when manager Karpen banned Pennebaker from filming them unless he paid a fee. Instead, Pennebaker shot footage of the crowd during Big Brother's set, capturing singer Cass Elliot's blissed-out reaction.

With Big Brother and the Holding Company, San Francisco, 1967

Thankfully, their performance was so rapturously received, they were invited to play again the following night. This time Pennebaker's cameras would have full access. The Sunday line-up included The Who at their auto-destructive finest, the Grateful Dead, The Mamas and the Papas and, making their debut at a major US event, The Jimi Hendrix Experience. Daunting company indeed.

Simply Mesmerizing

If Janis was intimidated by the star wattage of the Sunday night bill, there's not a trace of it in her performance – or at least the fragment of it that featured in Pennebaker's film. Decked out in a gold-embroidered tunic and matching flares, her hair a witchy halo, she belts out an emotional version of Big Mamma Thornton's 'Ball and Chain' that is simply mesmerizing. For those few moments, the Monterey stage is hers and hers alone, and the crowd is in the palm of her hand. Only Hendrix's spectacular sonic onslaught gave her any competition – and he had to set his guitar on fire to do it. That night, Janis at once announced herself as a rock star, and laid the foundations for our understanding of what a rock star is.

Things began to change quickly for Big Brother after Monterey. Their eponymous debut album was rushed out in August

'[Janis] more than anyone else at Monterey made me intensely aware and excited about the new and future direction of music.'

CLIVE DAVIS, PRESIDENT OF COLUMBIA RECORDS

At home, San Francisco, 1967

'I just want to feel as much as I can, it's what soul is all about.' JANIS JOPLIN

Ingredient X

This can't have surprised anyone. An uncomfortable truth, laid bare by Joplin's performance at Monterey, is that Big Brother were not quite up to the job. They weren't a terrible band, far from it, but apart from Sam Andrew's piercing lead guitar (which itself couldn't hold a candle to Jorma Kaukonen's playing on the 'Typewriter Tape'), they just didn't have enough of the all-important Ingredient X, which like other magic potions in 1967 San Francisco, was in otherwise abundant supply.

to capitalize on the buzz and, substandard though it was, it boosted their profile enormously across the country. Towards the end of the year, Columbia took over the band's contract and re-issued the album, adding two previously released singles recorded in LA in 1966, 'Coo Coo' and 'The Last Time'. They also modified the title. It was now *Big Brother and the Holding Company Featuring Janis Joplin*.

In February 1968, the band began their first tour of the East Coast with gigs in Boston and New York. On 7 April, they appeared with Jimi Hendrix, Joni Mitchell, B.B. King, Buddy Guy and Richie Havens at the Wake for Martin Luther King Jr concert in New York. Their official billing was now Janis Joplin and Big Brother and the Holding Company.

Golden Gate Park, 1 January 1969

'Don't compromise yourself. It's all you've got.'

JANIS JOPLIN

1967: Riding A Carousel

Janis met Country Joe McDonald of Country Joe and the Fish in February 1967 when they were both booked to play a concert at the Golden Sheaf Bakery in Berkeley, California. After breaking up with Rivers, she moved in with Country Joe, sharing a house with him on a residential street in the Haight. The affair didn't last long; few of Janis's dalliances did.

'Probably the most powerful singer to emerge from the white rock movement.'

TIME

With Big Brother and the Holding Company, Fillmore East, New York, 1968

with an African-American woman named Jae Whitaker, and had a longstanding, on-off relationship with Haight-Ashbury boutique owner Peggy Caserta who, to keep things interesting, was also in love with Big Brother guitarist Sam Andrew.

As her fame snowballed and her public persona crystalized, Joplin cultivated the image of a free-wheeling, hard-partying sexual predator. She wore garish feather boas in her hair, renounced underwear and sported her ever-present bottle of Southern Comfort like a chic accessory. She did so much to popularize the brand, in fact, she was able to wheedle a fur coat out of them.

Keeping It Interesting

Over the next few years, she had a string of lovers that included the Grateful Dead's Ron 'Pigpen' McKernan, Kris Kristofferson and Leonard Cohen, who wrote the song 'Chelsea Hotel #2' in her honour. It's also been suggested – with good reason – that she had an affair with American TV talk show host Dick Cavett, who interviewed her several times and plainly adored her. During her first stint in San Francisco, she lived for a while

'A mixture of Lead Belly, a steam engine, Calamity Jane, Bessie Smith, an oil derrick and rot-gut bourbon…'

CASH BOX

'Man, if it hadn't been for the music, I probably would have done myself in.' **JANIS JOPLIN**

With Big Brother and the Holding Company, Generation, New York, April 1968

New Album

The band toured extensively in the early months of 1968, and in March began recording sessions for a new album at Columbia's Studio E in Manhattan. The in-house producer was John Simon, who had graduated from Broadway cast recordings and an LP of Senator Joseph McCarthy's anti-Communist Senate hearings to producing debut albums for Leonard Cohen and Blood, Sweat & Tears. Although still relatively inexperienced, Simon was an infinitely better fit than Bob Shad.

Emotionally Brutal

By now, Janis was receiving massive media attention, a state of affairs that magnified the gradually widening gap between her and the band. On one side there were dark mutterings that she was on a 'star trip' and that they had already been demoted to her backing group. On the other were insinuations that Big Brother were a second-rate outfit and that she'd be better off without them. With Janis caught in the middle, this can't have helped the atmosphere in the studio. Even so, according to Simon, Janis was entirely professional, the first to arrive at the studio in the morning and the last to leave at

'As it gets closer and more probable, being a star is really losing its meaning.'

JANIS JOPLIN

Fillmore East, New York, 1968

night. She played a crucial role in arranging and producing the songs, which included 'Ball And Chain', 'Turtle Blues' and a show-stopping cover of the Erma Franklin hit 'Piece Of My Heart', transformed by Joplin into an emotionally brutal howl of pain and defiance.

Footage of her in the studio, recording the Gershwin classic 'Summertime', shows her on winning form, orchestrating proceedings with humour and authority. At the end of the clip, she glances sidelong at the camera, raises a quizzical eyebrow, then winks and grins. It's a thoroughly captivating moment.

Star Trip

The band's proposed title for the album was *Sex, Dope and Cheap Thrills*. Needless to say, this was quickly overruled by Columbia and the more succinct – and, let's be honest, better – *Cheap Thrills* was settled on. Mistaken by many for a live recording, *Cheap Thrills* stays remarkably true to the rawness of the band and to Joplin's bravura singing. Only one track, 'Ball and Chain', was actually recorded live, but crowd noise was added to the mix on 'Combination Of The Two' and 'I Need A Man To Love'. Elsewhere, a glass can be heard smashing in the background.

Columbia's original concept for the cover was a portrait of Joplin. Rather contradicting the 'star trip' accusations, she flatly refused, insisting that the back cover illustration, by underground comic book artist R. Crumb, should take pride of place. According to Columbia Records' art director John Berg, Joplin herself commissioned the piece and Crumb, unwilling to sully his hands with Columbia's 'filthy lucre', refused payment.

Bestseller

The album was a huge hit. Released in the summer of 1968, it reached No. 1 on the *Billboard* charts and held the top spot for eight (non-consecutive) weeks. It sold over a million copies, ending the year as the best-selling album of 1968. Reviews, however, were mixed. John Hardin of *Rolling Stone* was bluntly

Fillmore East, New York, 1968

critical, proclaiming it no better than the previous year's lacklustre effort. Writing in *Esquire*, Robert Christgau was more positive. 'It not only gets Janis's voice down,' he wrote, 'it also does justice to her always underrated and ever-improving musicians.'

Still, the phrase 'ever-improving' smacks of damning with faint praise, and the reference to Big Brother as 'her'

musicians is telling. Buoyed by the success of the premiere of the concert documentary *Monterey Pop* in December 1968, *Cheap Thrills* propelled Joplin to the forefront of celebrity, its success serving, ironically, to drive the wedge ever deeper between her and the band.

1968: Thrills And Spills

Summer 1968 was a busy one for the band, with another tour of the East coast, playing the Columbia Records Convention in San Juan, Puerto Rico, and the annual Newport Folk Festival in Newport, Rhode Island, in July.

Number One

'Piece Of My Heart', the lead single from *Cheap Thrills*, was released in the US in August of 1968. It became Joplin's biggest hit during her lifetime and her gut-wrenching, no-holds-barred rendition is still revered as the definitive version. It steadily climbed the charts, eventually peaking at No. 12.

Going Solo

Following two shows at the Palace of Fine Arts in San Francisco on 31 August and 1 September, Joplin put an end to the hubbub

At Ratner's restaurant, New York, 1969

Aragon Ballroom, Chicago, August 1968

of rumour and speculation by announcing that she was leaving Big Brother to pursue a solo career. It was, according to manager Albert Grossman, an 'amicable split.' A concert on 14 September, at the historic music venue Fillmore West, was heavily publicized by promoter Bill Graham as Janis's last appearance with the band. Naturally, the show was a sell-out, but it didn't quite live up to its billing. Janis continued on as lead singer for several months, playing gigs in Vancouver, New York, Chicago, Puerto Rico and Los Angeles. Her final official performance with Big Brother and the Holding Company was in San Francisco on 1 December 1968, a benefit for her old mentor and ex-manager Chet Helms. Less than three weeks later, she was rehearsing with a new band.

With Kozmic Blues Band, Memphis, December 1968

Staying Clean

When Janis returned to San Francisco in 1966, she was determined to stay clean of drugs. While sharing an apartment with Travis Rivers, she made him promise it would be a needle-free zone and, on one occasion, became hysterical when she walked in on a group of Rivers' friends injecting methadone. It was a valiant effort but, given her personality and the central role drugs played in the counterculture, to say nothing of their sheer availability, it was doomed to fail. In a matter of months, she was using heroin again. By the time she parted ways with Big Brother, she was already battling a fatal addiction.

A Blast Of Indifference

The new band, an ersatz soul/R&B outfit with keyboards and a horn section, got off to a shaky start. Christened The Kozmic Blues Band (KBB), their first engagement was at the Stax/Volt 'Yuletide Thing' concert in Memphis, organized by Stax Records president Jim Stewart. The rest of the bill comprised blues legend Albert King and Stax stablemates the Bar-Kays (Otis Redding's backing band), The Mad Lads, Rufus and Carla Thomas, Judy Clay and Eddie Floyd. In that company, and despite a last-minute rehearsal the night before, KBB were ill-prepared and out of their

First Kozmic Blues Band performance, Memphis, December 1968

'I'm one of those regular weird people.'

JANIS JOPLIN

Memphis, December 1968

depth. Not even Janis's star power could win over the audience to enjoy some hardcore Memphis soul, never mind a hastily assembled facsimile of it. The band left the stage to a smattering of applause and a sobering blast of indifference.

Janis was inconsolable. A central tenet of Janis mythology is that her brash public image camouflaged deep insecurities and fear of failure. Whether that's true or not – and opinion from people who knew her varies – there's no doubt that she was, at her core, a sensitive soul who would've been deeply wounded by the crowd's reaction that night. It's not hard to imagine where she sought solace.

'The whole Janis Joplin hype has grown to outrageous proportions, whereby impossible goals have been established for her.'

ROLLING STONE

High Expectations

With the Kozmic Blues Band's New York debut at the Fillmore fast approaching, Grossman made efforts to whip them into shape. He arranged an out-of-town try-out in Rindge, New Hampshire (the most obscure booking he could find), before they played the Fillmore on 11 and 12 February 1969. Lacklustre reviews for the Memphis show had done nothing to dim Janis's celebrity, and expectations among fans and the media were running vertiginously high for the New York shows. Once again, they were not met. It was an improvement over Memphis, but the overall vibe stubbornly refused to gel. A 1970 article in *Rolling Stone* was, perhaps, on the money when it noted that: 'The distance between singer and band had never been more apparent.'

Not Impressed

Now firmly established as the lurid embodiment of the counterculture itself (in the public imagination at least), Janis was launched on an interstellar star trip whether she liked it or not. On 18 March, the Kozmic Blues Band appeared on *The Ed Sullivan Show*, conclusive proof that they had 'arrived'. No prizes for guessing who the main attraction was. And despite the KBB's underwhelming track record so far, Grossman was able to charge extortionate appearance fees purely on the back of their lead singer. Neither fans nor critics were impressed. Following their first hometown show at the Fillmore West on 23 March, *San Francisco Chronicle* columnist Ralph J. Gleason wrote: 'The best things that could be done would be for her to scrap this band and go right back to being a member of Big Brother ... If they'll have her.'

'She was open and spontaneous enough to get her heart trampled with a regularity that took me 30 years to experience or understand.'

GRACE SLICK

1969: Going Kosmic

'They're paying me fifty thousand dollars a year to be like me,' crowed Janis, at the height of her fame, revelling in the novelty of celebrity and the perks that came with it. It might be putting too fine a point on it, but it is interesting that she said 'to be like me' not 'to be me'. In truth, the fifty grand was for the most outlandish aspects of herself, and only then when played to the hilt.

'There was no bullshit with Janis, she was the real deal. She was an original, a pure soul.'

JORMA KAUKONEN

Royal Albert Hall, London, April 1969

'You know why we're stuck with the myth that only black people have soul? Because white people don't let themselves feel things.'

JANIS JOPLIN

JJ, 1969

An Honest Rock Star

There wasn't a fake bone in Joplin's body. She was, perhaps, the most nakedly honest rock star in history, but she was smart enough to know how the game was played and that, for all she was touted as the pinup girl of proto-feminism, the music business was still a rigidly defined patriarchy; as, after all, was the counterculture itself. Janis embraced the concept of free love as enthusiastically as anyone, but she knew that real freedom for women, even one in her position, was strictly limited. 'She had less room to manoeuvre than a man in her position,' Ellen Willis puts it in *Rolling Stone*. '[And] fewer alternatives to fall back on if she blew it.'

A Blind Alley

There was no danger of Janis blowing it, not yet at any rate. But the new direction she'd taken since leaving Big Brother seemed more of a blind alley than a fresh start. The band, made up of seasoned session players like keyboardist Stephen Ryder and saxophonist Cornelius 'Snooky' Flowers, were, on paper, musically superior to Big Brother. In practice, however, they didn't have the pizzazz to pull off the Stax/Volt sound Joplin was looking for. For all their

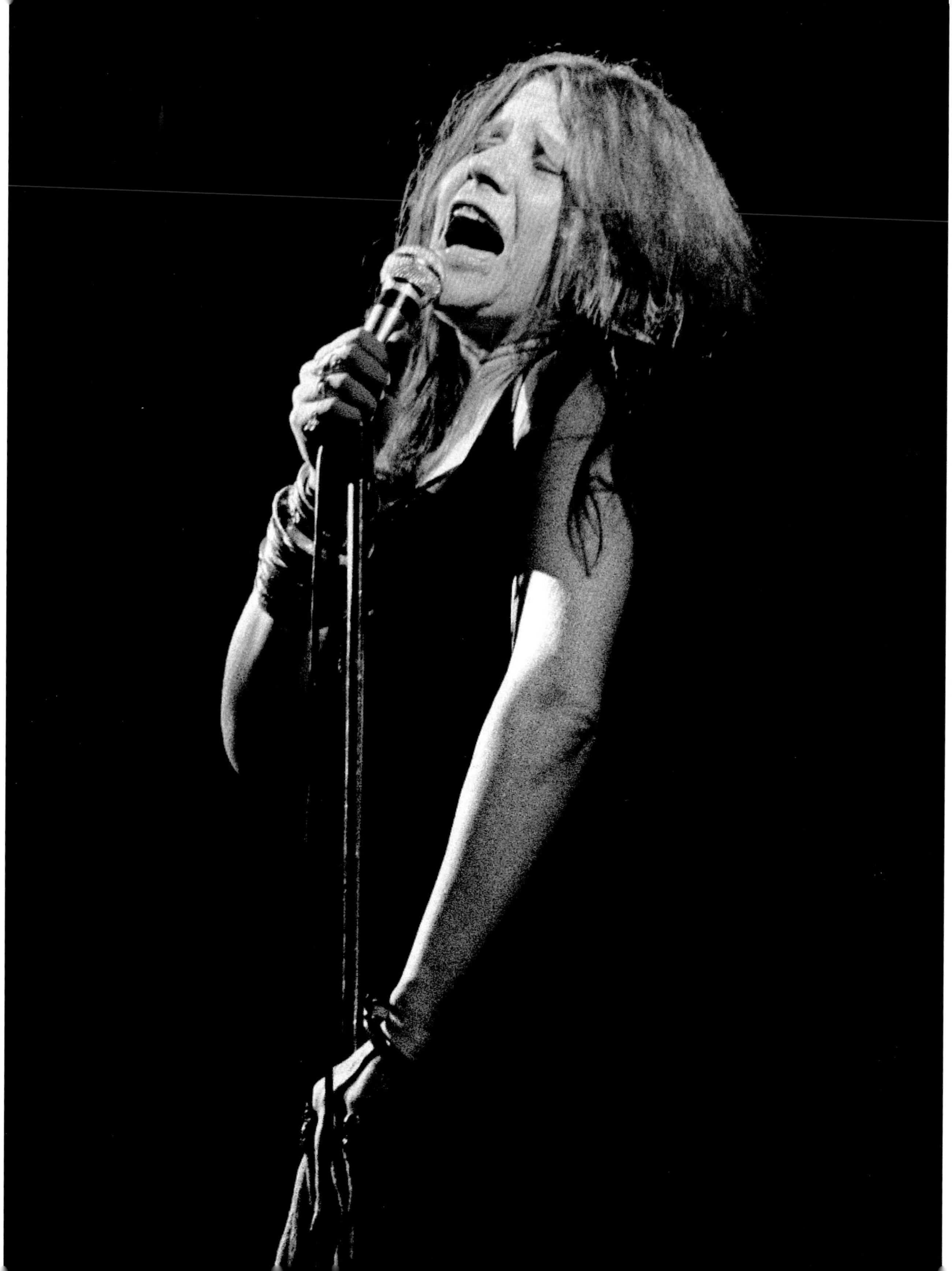

Fillmore East, New York, February 1969

shortcomings, Big Brother were a band and they played like one. Sacrilegious though it may sound, there were also mutterings that, on occasion, Joplin's vocals were veering towards the histrionic.

Rave Reviews

In April 1969, Janis and the Kozmic Blues Band kicked off a tour of Europe with a concert in Frankfurt that was filmed for the German TV documentary *Janis*. Live footage shows the band in good form, as well as scenes of mayhem towards the end of the show as the audience floods the stage unencumbered by security, since, for some reason, no one had thought to hire any. The KBB later played in Stockholm, Amsterdam, Paris, Copenhagen and at the Albert Hall in London, Janis's one and only appearance in the UK. Her performance earned rave reviews from the local and national press and from weekly music paper *Melody Maker*. Several weeks later, *Melody Maker* ran an interview with her, in which she complained bitterly, and hilariously, about being bumped from the cover of *Newsweek* by the death of President Dwight D. Eisenhower. 'God-dammit you mother-#&!3!,' she rails. 'Fourteen heart attacks and he had to die in my week. In MY week!'

'Janis is a curiosity as well as a musical attraction.'

JOHN HUDDY, *COLUMBUS DISPATCH*

Los Angeles, 1969

'Madame Of Rock'

On 11 May, Janis turned in her best performance with so far KBB at Veterans Memorial Auditorium in Columbus, Ohio, prompting a fulsome outpouring of praise from *Columbus Dispatch* critic John Huddy. He wrote: 'She cultivates a Madame of Rock image, lounging against an organ, exchanging profanities with bandsmen, cackling coarsely at private jokes, even taking a belt or two … She also has something to say in her songs, about the raw and rudimentary dimensions of sex, love and life. She gets her point across, splitting a few eardrums in the process.'

'Janis seems bent on becoming Aretha Franklin.'

RALPH J. GLEASON

In June, recording sessions for a Kozmic Blues album began at Columbia studios in Hollywood. According to folklore, the band may or may not have played at the semi-legendary Newport 69 Festival held on 20–22 June in Northridge, California. Some attendees – never the most reliable witnesses when it comes to 1960s rock festivals – claim they didn't, others claim they did, even reporting an impromptu duet between Janis and headliner Jimi Hendrix. They weren't on the official bill but, again, that proves nothing.

A Dangerous Addiction

The same month, Janis made her first appearance on *The Dick Cavett Show*. The band played 'Try (Just A Little Bit Harder)' and 'To Love Somebody', and Janis, in a one-to-one interview, visibly charmed the pants off Cavett, an altogether more erudite and sophisticated host than Ed Sullivan. During the interview Janis describes the 'terrible' time she had touring Europe, thanks to uptight audiences and their inability to 'get down'.

Whatever she might have told Cavett in private, the real reason for her terrible time in Europe wasn't suitable for broadcast. By early 1969, Janis's heroin habit was costing her $200 a day (around $1,400 in today's money). Throughout the tour she had approached every international border in a cold sweat, knowing that if they were discovered by customs officials, the drugs she had hidden on her person would land her in a foreign jail for years. However, her addiction was so acute by this point, she judged it worth the risk.

1969: First Lady Of Rock

Throughout the recording of the Kozmic Blues Band's debut album, Janis was living under virtual house arrest at record producer Gabriel Mekler's home in Los Angeles, a vain yet well-intentioned attempt to keep her away from heroin.

Mixed Reviews

The album, clumsily titled *I Got Dem Ol' Kozmic Blues Again Mama!,* was released in September 1969 to predictably mixed reviews. In general, it was deemed a better record than *Cheap Thrills* in terms of musicianship and production, but it didn't have Big Brother's raw edge or live spontaneity. A pre-Watergate-busting Carl Bernstein wrote a positive, if rather fusty review in *The Washington Post*: '[Joplin] has finally assembled a group of first-rate musicians … whose abilities complement the incredible range of her voice.' Ralph J. Gleason, of the *San Francisco Chronicle*, was never the KBB's biggest fan, and was less kind

WOODSTOCK MUSIC & ART FAIR presents AN AQUARIAN EXPOSITION in WHITE LAKE, N.Y.

WITH

FRI. AUG. 15
Joan Baez
Arlo Guthrie
Tim Hardin
Richie Havens
Incredible String Band
Ravi Shankar
Sly And The Family Stone
Bert Sommer
Sweetwater

SAT. AUG. 16
Canned Heat
Creedence Clearwater
Grateful Dead
Keef Hartley
Janis Joplin
Jefferson Airplane
Mountain
Quill
Santana
The Who

SUN. AUG. 17
The Band
Jeff Beck Group
Blood, Sweat and Tears
Joe Cocker
Crosby, Stills and Nash
Jimi Hendrix
Iron Butterfly
Ten Years After
Johnny Winter

ART SHOW

CRAFTS BAZAAR

FOOD

HUNDREDS OF ACRES TO ROAM ON

MUSIC STARTS AT 4:00 P.M. ON FRIDAY, AND AT 1:00 P.M. ON SATURDAY AND SUNDAY.

AUGUST 15, 16, 17

3 DAYS OF PEACE & MUSIC

*WHITE LAKE, TOWN OF BETHEL, SULLIVAN COUNTY, N.Y.

and less wordy. He dismissed the band as 'a drag.' The album was certified gold later in the year and reached No. 5 on the *Billboard 200* chart, but sales were disappointing compared to *Cheap Thrills*.

A Defining Moment

Prior to the album release, on 3 August 1969, Janis confirmed her status as rock'n'roll royalty (if confirmation was needed) by singing a duet with Little Richard at the Atlantic City Pop Festival in New Jersey. On 17 August, she performed in front of 400,000 people at the Woodstock Music and Art Fair in Bethel, New York, the mother of all rock festivals and a defining moment of the 1960s. With the Summer of Love two years in the past, and the death-knell horror of Altamont Festival waiting around the corner, Woodstock was hippiedom's last glorious, shambolic hurrah.

Accompanied by her on-and-off lover Peggy Caserta, Joplin flew into the festival site by helicopter, giddily surveying the vast ocean of people below. On landing, she was raring to go and was due to appear later that afternoon. Instead, she had to wait for 10 hours while band after band ran late. To kill time, she and Caserta drank and shot heroin. The Kozmic Blues Band finally took the stage around 2 a.m.

Woodstock Music and Art Fair, 1969

J.J. c. 1969

Blowsy But Heartfelt

It is a tribute to Joplin's stamina and professionalism that, after a 10-hour smack and Southern Comfort binge, she could still put on a credible, even heroic show. Woodstock was not her finest hour by any means – her voice was hoarse and she was none too steady on her feet – but her titanic charisma and sheer talent carried the day. At the end of her set, the crowd demanded an encore. They were rewarded with a blowsy but heartfelt rendition of 'Ball And Chain'. The Who's Pete Townsend, who played later

'The mark of great talent, creative talent and original talent is also in its difficulty to copy that talent. And I think that's what Janis has.'

BILL GRAHAM, CONCERT PROMOTER

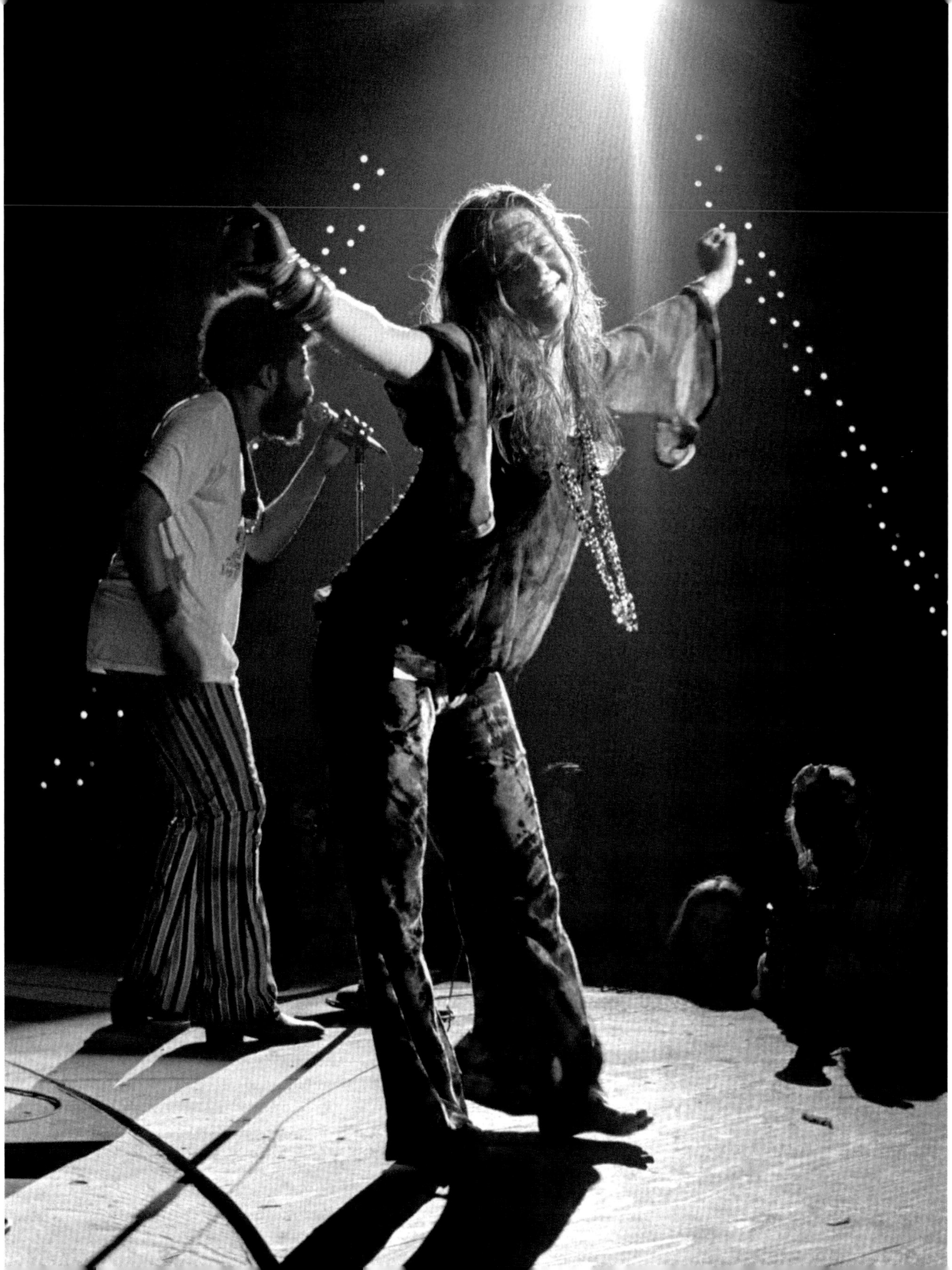

Woodstock, August 1969

Asbury Park Convention Hall, New Jersey, August 1969

'Vulgar And Obscene'

During late August and into September, the band played a string of major events, including the Texas International Pop Festival in Lewisville, the New Orleans Pop Festival in Baton Rouge, Louisiana, and a headlining spot at the Hollywood Bowl in Los Angeles. Following a month of relative inactivity, they hit the road again in November to support the release of the *Kozmic Blues* album. On 16 November, Janis was charged with two counts of using vulgar and obscene language during a concert at Curtis Hixon Hall in Tampa, Florida. Censuring Janis Joplin for swearing is a little like issuing speeding tickets at the Monaco Grand Prix, but the charge stuck and she was later fined $200.

the same morning, summed things up succinctly in his 2012 autobiography: 'She wasn't at her best ... But even Janis on an off night was incredible.' Janis disagreed. Blaming Caserta, she was so dissatisfied with her performance she insisted it wasn't included in either the 1970 documentary film of the festival or on the best-selling soundtrack album.

Directly after Woodstock, Sam Andrew, who had left Big Brother to join Janis in the Kozmic Blues Band, quit. He would later rejoin Big Brother.

'People have a certain perfection about them, no matter who they are. Like when Janis Joplin sang.'

JEFF BUCKLEY

'Man, I'd rather have ten years

of superhypermost than live

to be seventy sitting in some

goddamn chair watching

television.'

JANIS JOPLIN

Cursing like a stevedore, on stage and off, was business as usual for Janis. In other respects, however, her behaviour was becoming increasingly troubling, even by her standards. It was, as much as anything, force of personality that got her through Woodstock and presumably through subsequent performances. But not even a personality as strong as Janis's could outrun a $200-a-day heroin habit indefinitely.

'I just loved Amy Winehouse ... To me, it was like the first time I saw Janis Joplin.'

JERRY HELLER

Is She Gonna Make It?

On 27 November, Thanksgiving Day, she made a surprise appearance on stage at Madison Square Garden in New York to sing a number with Tina Turner, who was opening for the

With Tina Turner, Madison Square Garden, November 1969

Rider College, Trenton, New Jersey, November 1969

Rolling Stones. The event was witnessed by her biographer Myra Freidman, who later wrote: '[Janis was] so drunk, so stoned, so out of control that she could have been an institutionalized psychotic rent by mania.' During another concert at the Garden on 19 December, she broadcast her sexual encounter with American football star Joe Namath and, some observers believe, attempted to incite the crowd to riot. She told writer David Dalton in a 1970 interview that the audience that night had hung on 'every note with "is she gonna make it" in their eyes.' They were, perhaps, not confining their concern to the concert.

'If I hold back, I'm no good *now,* and I'd rather be good sometimes than holding back all the time.'

JANIS JOPLIN

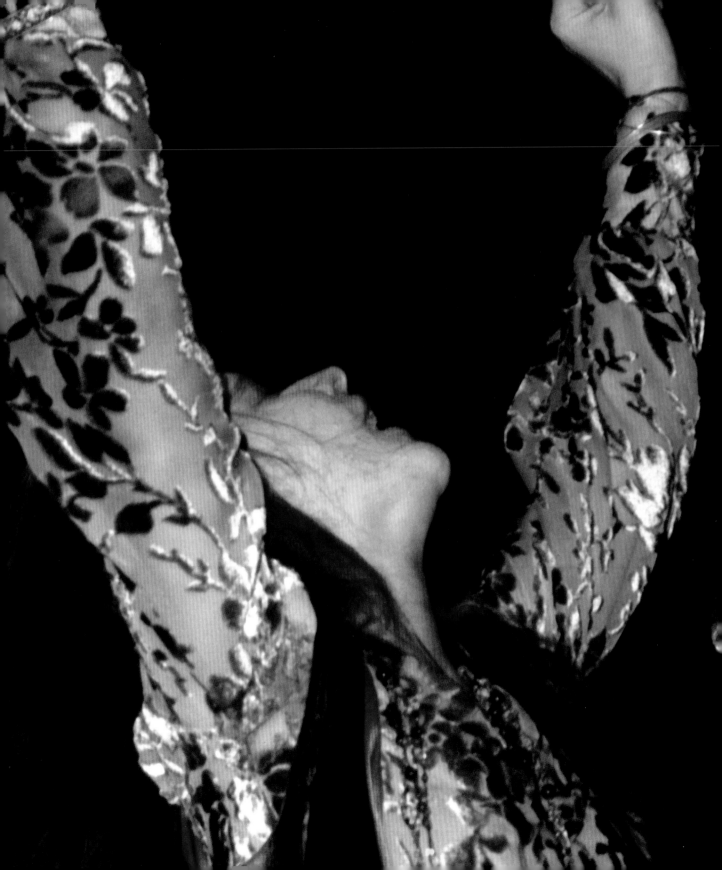

1970: At Full Tilt

The Madison Square Garden concert on 19 December was the last time the Kozmic Blues Band performed live. They officially disbanded in January 1970, unlamented on the whole, but leaving a handful of highlights and a respectable album in their wake. Despite the break-up, Janis began the new decade in a positive frame of mind. In February, she flew to Rio de Janeiro for the Carnival celebrations and was, she said, planning a long vacation 'to get off drugs and dry out'.

With Gerry Garcia, Festival Express, June/July 1970

The Straight And Narrow

While in Brazil, Joplin began a romantic relationship with David Niehaus, a law school drop-out from Cincinnati who had worked for the Peace Corp in Turkey and was now travelling the world. An odd couple, even with Janis clean, they nevertheless hit it off in a big way. Photos of them at the Rio Carnival reveal an outwardly happy, well-adjusted young couple enjoying the celebrations and

'On stage I make love to 25,000 people, and then I go home alone.'

JANIS JOPLIN

each other's company immensely. For now, at least, Janis was on the straight and narrow. 'The nicest thing about David was that he wasn't into drugs,' wrote Ellis Amburn in his 1992 book *Pearl*: *The Obsessions and Passions of Janis Joplin*.

'This Is My Band!'

In April, Janis took the lead in forming her third and final group. The Kozmic Blues had been put together largely without her input, and Big Brother and the Holding Company were, of course, an established unit before she joined. Things were different with

'This band is solid, their sound is so heavy you could lean on it, and that means I can go further out, and extend myself.'

JANIS JOPLIN

Brazil, 1970

'You could say that being yelled at by Janis Joplin was one of the great honors of my life.'

STEVIE NICKS

the Full Tilt Boogie Band, as she christened them. 'Finally, this is *my* band,' she crowed. Confident that the next chapter of her career was under way, and to show there were no hard feelings, she re-united with Big Brother for a gig at the Fillmore West in San Francisco on 4 April and again on 12 April at the Winterland Ballroom. Two tracks from the Fillmore show, 'All Is Loneliness' and 'Ego Rock', surfaced on the 1972 live album *In Concert*.

The Full Tilt Boogie Band made their first live appearance in May 1970 on the same bill as Big Brother, at a Hell's Angels party in San Rafael, California. According to Sam Andrew, the atmosphere was tense, and accounts of Janis's performance that night are wildly at odds. Big Brother lead singer Nick Gravenites (who had helped put the Kozmic Blues Band together) deemed

With the Full Tilt Boogie Band, 1970

her singing 'stupendous'. Andrew was of a very different opinion. Twenty years later, interviewed by Ellis Amburn, he described her as bloated and visibly deteriorating, a parody of past glories, her singing 'flabby' and lacking edge. He put it down to her excessive drinking. Janis may have kicked heroin, but she'd upped her consumption of liquor to compensate. 'I felt a tinge of fear for her wellbeing,' said Andrew.

Engaging And Saucy

When the band set out on the Festival Express train tour through Canada that summer, Janis confirmed Andrew's suspicions, telling people she was off heroin but drinking more Southern Comfort than ever. Her 28 June appearance on the Dick Cavett show, three days before the tour began, reveals her as pale and a little blurred around the edges, but generally as engaging and saucy as ever. And her claims to be drug free were, for the moment, nothing less than the truth. In sharp contrast to her experiences in Europe, when she arrived at the Canadian border for the start of the Express tour, she actively encouraged officials to search her bags, regarding their efforts with amusement. She was delighted when one of them dug out a bag of suspicious-looking white powder and held it up to her quizzically. 'That's douche powder, honey,' she hollered, gleefully.

Harvard Stadium, Boston, August 1970

'Little Songbird'

Concerts in Hawaii, San Diego, New York and Austin (where she sang at a birthday party for Ken Threadgill) followed. On 3 August 1970, Janis made her third and final appearance on *The Dick Cavett Show*. This time, much as Sam Andrew had described her, she looked pasty and a little bloated. But their conversation was loose and amiable, and there was obviously a great deal of affection between them (Cavett greets her as: 'My little songbird.')

'To see the person she was turning into, it was clear there was some sort of tragic unfulfilment about her.'

JORMA KAUKONEN

Oh Lord…

In August, Joplin paid a moving tribute to Bessie Smith, her greatest inspiration. She and Juanita Green, who had done housework for Smith as a child – and was now president of the North Philadelphia chapter of the National Association for the Advancement of Colored People (NAACP) – paid for a headstone to be laid at Smith's grave, which had been left unmarked since her death in a road accident in 1937. The inscription read: 'The Greatest Blues Singer In The World Will Never Stop Singing.'

Bessie Smith headstone, Mount Lawn Cemetery, Sharon Hill, Pennsylvania

THE GREATEST BLUES SINGER
IN THE WORLD WILL NEVER
STOP SINGING
BESSIE SMITH
1895 —— 1937

On 8 August, at a concert in Port Chester, New York, Joplin sang the song 'Mercedes Benz' for the first time, having written the lyrics with her friend, folk singer Bob Neuwirth, in a bar next to the theatre earlier that day. On 12 August 1970, Janis and the Full Tilt Boogie Band played at Harvard Stadium in Boston. It would be her last ever live performance. The following day, she flew to Port Arthur to attend her high school reunion.

1970: Bye Bye Baby

Janis's return to Port Arthur was not a joyful homecoming. Hounded by the press, she took the opportunity to badmouth the town and its inhabitants. When asked by a reporter whether she'd entertained her classmates at Thomas Jefferson High, she replied acidly: 'Only when I walked down the aisles.' If her aim was to rub her superstar status in the faces of her former detractors, she succeeded magnificently.

An Exotic Creature

Dressed in gold-embroidered purple satin, with painted toenails, feathers in her hair and, as *Rolling Stone* put it, 'rings and bracelets enough for a Babylonian whore', she must have seemed to the locals like some exotic creature loose in their midst – and a venomous one at that. She and her entourage commandeered the bar of the town's Goodhue Hotel, Janis imperiously sending a flunky for vodka when told they didn't stock it.

JJ, 1970

'She had a lot of needs that were just like everyone else's.'

MYRA FRIEDMAN, JOPLIN'S PUBLICIST

On 24 August 1970, Janis checked into the Landmark Motor Hotel on Franklin Avenue in Hollywood. She was in Los Angeles to record an album with the Full Tilt Boogie Band and producer Paul A. Rothchild, famed for his work with The Doors. Although hardly luxurious, the Landmark was a firm favourite with musicians, partly for its proximity to the recording studios on Sunset Boulevard, but mostly for its staff, whose twin virtues were absolute discretion and a high tolerance for debauchery. Sad as it is to say, it was the perfect place for Janis, who had once again relapsed into addiction, her habit quickly sabotaging her relationship with David Niehaus, who left her – apparently with some reluctance – to continue his travels.

JJ, c. 1970

'I think she really sums up the idea that soul is about putting your pain into something beautiful.'

FLORENCE WELCH, FLORENCE AND THE MACHINE

A New Dress, A New Man

Still, as late summer turned to autumn, friends reported that Janis was happier than she'd been in a while. The recording sessions were going well and, with Niehaus gone, she had another man in her life. John Carpenter, music editor of the *Los Angeles Free Press*, saw her briefly at The Troubadour nightclub, on 28 September. 'She said she "had a lover now" and seemed cheerful,' he recalled. 'She had a red dress on and I asked her what she was doing there. She said "I got this new dress and I just wanted to look good."'

The lover in question was a fellow free spirit named Seth Morgan, the future author of cult novel *Homeboy*, who had dropped out of University of California, Berkeley, earlier in the year and had, allegedly, met Joplin while delivering cocaine to her home. She confided to close friends that she and Morgan were engaged.

Taking Care Of Business

On 1 October, Joplin visited her attorney Robert Gordon to discuss what Gordon later described as 'business matters'. 'She seemed very happy,' he said. 'She told me she was thinking of getting married.' They also discussed the album and her singing, both of which Janis was enthusiastic about. She also told Gordon that a tour was scheduled for November. When pressed on exactly what the 'business matters' were, Gordon replied: 'I might as well tell you. She signed her will.'

'Janis would give everything. And after you give everything, what do you do when the audience wants more?'

KIP COHEN,
MANAGER OF THE FILLMORE EAST

FINAL ★★★★

DAILY NEWS
NEW YORK'S PICTURE NEWSPAPER ®

10¢

Vol. 52. No. 87 — New York, N.Y. 10017, Monday, October 5, 1970* — WEATHER: Sunny and cool

JANIS JOPLIN IS FOUND DEAD
— Story on Page 5

Tombs Rebels Free Hostages

A First-Hand Report. As helmeted policemen stand by, Mayor Lindsay speaks with press after his arrival from Gracie Mansion at the Tombs last night, following release of 17 hostages by rebellious inmates. Lindsay then went inside to speak with prisoners. Earlier, he had issued an ultimatum to prisoners to release hostages. —Stories p.3

Names of Eligible Winners in Million Dollar Lottery—Page 38

'To have one of our peers go like that, it was a reality check to all of us.'

JORMA KAUKONEN

Love You Mama

On Saturday 3 October, Janis finished a recording session then spent time with some bandmates at Barney's Beanery bar in West Hollywood before returning to her hotel. The last person to see her alive was Jack Hagy, the hotel manager, who spoke to her briefly around 1 a.m. on Sunday 4 October.

The following day she was due at the studio to record vocals for the track 'Buried Alive In The Blues'. When she failed to appear, John Cooke, the band's road manager, drove to the Landmark. The first thing he saw was Janis's psychedelically painted Porsche in the parking lot.

When he entered her room, he found her body, dressed in a short nightgown, wedged between the bed and the nightstand. Her lips were bloody and her nose was broken. She was clutching $4.50 in her right hand.

The official cause of death was a heroin overdose, possibly confounded by alcohol. The next morning, a telegram turned up at the Landmark from David Niehaus. It read: 'Love you Mama, more than you know …'

Raise Your Hand

The album, titled *Pearl*, Joplin's nickname-come-alter-ego, was released on 11 January 1971. It reached No. 1 on the *Billboard* charts and stayed there for nine weeks. Joplin sang on nine of the album's ten tracks, all of which she personally arranged and approved. With the Boogie Band at full tilt, and Paul A. Rothchild manning the desk, it's a superbly crafted showcase for her phenomenal talent.

The Last Song

More polished, and still somehow more vibrant than anything she recorded with Big Brother or The Kozmic Blues Band, it has Janis's personality etched into every groove. Her voice is absent from only one track, an instrumental version of 'Buried Alive In The Blues', the song she was due to record the day she died. Nick Gravenites, who wrote it (and who replaced her as lead singer in Big Brother), was asked if he'd like to record the vocals as a tribute to Janis. Out of respect, he declined.

'Joplin belonged to that select group of pop figures who mattered as much for themselves as for their music.'

ELLEN WILLIS

JJ, 1970

Among the album's outstanding moments are Joplin's plaintive rendition of Kris Kristofferson and Fred Foster's 'Me and Bobby McGee' and her a cappella version of 'Mercedes Benz', the last song she ever recorded.

'A woman who inspired me when everyone else … didn't!'

PINK

The *Pearl* Sessions

Pearl was re-released by Columbia in 2012 as a two-disc set, boasting an abundance of additional tracks and retitled *The Pearl Sessions*. In the interim, every utterance that Janis committed to tape in the course of her life has made its way into the commercial market. Beginning with 1972's *In Concert*, around 20 albums, variously comprised of home demos, studio outtakes, live recordings, and repackaged existing tracks, have seen the light of day.

The Quiet Morning

Among the many songs dedicated to Janis are 'Pearl' by the Mamas and the Papas, 'Chelsea Hotel #2' by Leonard Cohen, 'Birdsong' by Jerry Garcia, and 'In The Quiet Morning' by

JJ. c. 1967

Mimi Farina, made famous by Joan Baez on her 1972 album *Come from the Shadows*. She was the subject of the 1975 documentary movie *Janis*, and in 1979, Bette Midler earned an Oscar nomination for her performance in *The Rose*, a thinly veiled Hollywood reimagining of her life and career. Several biopics of Joplin have been announced over the years, the most recent, with Michelle Williams in the lead role, is currently in production.

In May 1994, the stage musical *Love, Janis* by Randal Myler premiered at the Denver Center Theater. With musical direction by Big Brother guitarist Sam Andrew, it became an Off Broadway hit in 2001. In 2013, another stage production, *A Night with Janis Joplin*, opened at the Arena Stage in Washington DC.

Your Average Rock Icon

In 1995, Janis was inducted into the Rock & Roll Hall of Fame. In 2005, she received a Grammy Lifetime Achievement Award, and in 2014 was featured on a US Postal Service stamp. All run-of-the-mill for your average rock icon, but perhaps the most bizarre tribute to her came in 1995, when Mercedes-Benz began using her aspirational poke at consumerism in TV ads for their cars. Whatever Janis might have made of the other accolades piled at her feet, we can well imagine her reaction to that one.

Pearl

I n the summer of 1967 – the fabled Summer of Love – Big Brother and the Holding Company were big fish in a small pond. They played to full houses on the local circuit but were barely known outside of San Francisco. That changed on 17 June 1967, the moment they took to the stage at the Monterey International Pop Festival.

JJ, 1970

'The quality of our lives is diminished every time we lose a great artist. It's a different world without ... Janis Joplin.'

STEPHEN VAN ZANDT, GUITARIST

The Queen

The legendary gathering of musicians from across the globe at the Monterey International Pop Festival was a milestone event, the blueprint for all the festivals that followed and an opportunity for up-and-coming bands to broadcast their music to the world. Monterey turned the spotlight on the counterculture, illuminating the future of rock'n'roll. And no one, not even Jimi Hendrix making his – literally incendiary – North American debut, had more impact than Janis Joplin. She began her set as the lead singer of Big Brother but ended it a star in her own right.

JJ, 1969

'I think every woman ... owes Janis a lot. It's just a whole lot freer for women because Janis did the things she did.'

To put Joplin's appearance at Monterey in perspective, in 1967, the now-accepted figure of the rock star as demigod, the counterculture equivalent of Elvis Presley, was barely in its infancy. As charismatic as Mick Jagger and Jim Morrison were, they were still viewed as part of an ensemble, the frontman of a group rather than a solo performer with a backing band. With no intention of doing so, Janis changed that dynamic. Even before the band's name became Janis Joplin and Big Brother and the Holding Company, she had relegated them to the shadows. As film footage of her laying waste to Big Mamma Thornton's 'Ball And Chain' at Monterey amply demonstrates, she was the queen and they were her minions.

Spirit Of The Times

The image of Janis literally usurping Elvis's throne, left vacant when he joined the army, is irresistible – and it's not so far-fetched as a metaphor. Like Presley, Janis created a persona

'There are certain kinds of artists that blaze in a very bright light for a very brief time… And Janis was one of them.'

LEONARD COHEN

Janis Joplin

JJ, c. 1970

that contrived to capture the spirit of the times while remaining wholly unique. Even so, it was a long way from Graceland to the Haight, and the fact that Janis was a woman upped the ante even further. In stark contrast to Elvis and, in fact, to just about everyone else who had ever made a bid for stardom, especially women, Janis was not conventionally attractive; she had weight problems, bad skin and weird hair. That she not only invented her own beauty out of 'sheer energy, soul, sweetness, arrogance, and a sense of humor' (to quote writer Ellen Willis), and had that beauty appreciated, was a thumb

in the eye to the male-dominated music industry – the male-dominated world, come to that – and an early shot in a sexual revolution that was yet to get fully underway.

Lighting The Way

On another level entirely, Janis as a singer and performer opened the door for countless female pop stars who followed in her wake – Stevie Nicks, Patti Smith, Debbie Harry, Chrissie Hynde, PJ Harvey, Courtney Love and Amy Winehouse, to name a precious few. They might have had little in common with her musically and, with notable exceptions, shunned her outrageous lifestyle, but each of them, and many, many others, owe a debt to Joplin for lighting the way with such blazing passion. 'She sang in the great tradition of the rhythm and blues singers that were heroes,' said Stevie Nicks. 'But she brought her own dangerous, sexy rock'n'roll edge to every single song. And that inspired me to find my own voice and my own style.'

'She was the first lady of rock'n'roll, yet she did not have a role model.'

AMY BERG, FILM-MAKER

Tip Your Hat

As the first white artist who sang the blues with authenticity, her vocal talent was unsurpassed. And as much as anyone else from her era – Hendrix, Jim Morrison, Keith Richards – Joplin, with her peacock style, outlaw swagger, sexual appetites and hard-living lifestyle, created the rock star archetype, a powerful figure in modern folklore, now firmly implanted in the popular imagination as the epitome of f***-you cool.

The next time someone calls you a rock star, tip your hat to Janis Joplin. Dying tragically young, she was at least spared the ignomiy of fading away or drifting into grotesque self-parody, as Elvis did. But it is sad to reflect, nevertheless, that for Janis, and for too many others, the ultimate rock-star move was to check out of this life way, way too soon.

Further Information

Janis Joplin Vital Info

Birth Name: Janis Lyn Joplin

Born: 19 January 1943, Port Arthur, Texas

Died: 4 October 1970, Los Angeles, California

Role: Singer, songwriter

Discography
Janis Joplin In The Charts

Singles

Release	Title	US chart position
1966	'Blindman'	110
1967	'Down On Me'	43
1967	'Bye, Bye Baby'	118
1967	'Women Is Losers'	-
1968	'Coo Coo'	84
1968	'Piece Of My Heart'	12
1969	'Kozmic Blues'	41
1970	'Try (Just A Little Bit Harder)'	103
1970	'Maybe'	110
1971	'Me and Bobby McGee'	1
1971	'Cry Baby'	42
1971	'Get It While You Can'	78
1972	'Down On Me'	91

Compilations (selected)

Release	Title	US chart position
1972	Live In Concert	4
1973	Janis Joplin's Greatest Hits	37
1975	Janis	54
1975	The Great Janis	-
1977	Grand Prix 30	-
1980	Anthology	-
1982	Farewell Song	104
1984	Cheaper Thrills	-
1994	Woodstock Three Days of Peace and Music	-
1993	Janis	-
1995	18 Essential Songs	-
1995	This is Janis Joplin	-
1998	Winterland '68	-
1998	Janis Joplin: The Ultimate Collection (UK and Europe only)	
1999	Live at Woodstock, August 19, 1969	-
1999	Box of Pearls	
2000	Super Hits	113
2001	Love, Janis	-
2002	Live in San Francisco 1966	-
2003	Essential Janis Joplin	-
2004	The Collection	-
2007	Very Best of Janis Joplin	-
2008	The Lost Tapes	-
2009	The Woodstock Experience	-
2012	Live at the Carousel Ballroom 1968	-
2012	Blow All My Blues Away	-
2012	The Pearl Sessions	-
2016	Janis: Little Girl Blue	-
2018	Big Brother and the Holding Company – Sex, Dope, and Cheap Thrills	
2019	Woodstock – Back To The Garden 50th Anniversary Experience	-

Studio Albums

Release	Title	US chart position
With Big Brother and the Holding Company		
1967	*Big Brother and the Holding Company*	60
1968	*Cheap Thrills*	1
With Kozmic Blues Band		
1969	*I Got Dem Ol' Kozmic Blues Again Mama!*	5
With Full Tilt Boogie Band		
1971	*Pearl*	1

Accolades

1988 The Janis Joplin Memorial, a multi-image sculpture of Janis, is dedicated to her in Port Arthur, Texas, on what would have been her 45th birthday

1995 Inducted into the Rock & Roll Hall of Fame

2002 Janis's version of 'Me and Bobby McGee' inducted into the Grammy Hall of Fame

2005 Grammy Lifetime Achievement Award

2009 Honoured by the Rock & Roll Hall of Fame and Museum as part of its American Music Masters series

2009 Honoree at the Rock & Roll Hall of Fame's American Music Masters concert and lecture series

2010 Voted 23rd Greatest Singer of All Time, and 46th Greatest Artist of All Time by *Rolling Stone*

2012 *Cheap Thrills* added to the National Recording Registry of sound recordings deemed 'culturally, historically, or aesthetically important, and/or to inform or reflect life in the United States'

2013 Awarded 2510th star on the Hollywood Walk of Fame, located at 6752 Hollywood Boulevard

2013 Made for Pearl, a line of clothing and accessories inspired by Janis's sartorial style, launched. The line included replicas of her oversized round sunglasses, embroidered silk dresses and velvet bell-bottoms

2014 Portrait of Janis featured on a US Postal Service stamp as part of its Music Icons Forever series

2015 Subject of Amy J. Berg's documentary film *Janis: Little Girl Blue*, narrated by Cat Power, a *New York Times* Critics' Pick

Further Reading

Amburn, Ellis, *Pearl: The Obsessions and Passions of Janis Joplin* (Sphere, 1992)

Angel, Ann, *Janis Joplin: Rise Up Singing* (Amulet Books, 2010)

Burns, Pat, *Janis Joplin Snarky Coloring Book* (2019)

Byrne Cooke, John & Dalton, David, *Janis Joplin: A Performance Diary 1966-1970* (Art Data, 1997)

Byrne Cooke, John, *On the Road with Janis Joplin* (Berkley Books, 2014)

Caserta, Peggy & Knapp, Dan, *Going Down with Janis: A Raw and Scathing Portrait of Janis Joplin by Her Female Lover* (Futura Publications, 1974)

Echols, Alice, *Scars of Sweet Paradise: The Life and Times of Janis Joplin* (Virago, 2000)

Friedman, Myra, *Buried Alive: The Biography of Janis Joplin* (Plexus Publishing Ltd, 1989)

George-Warren, Holly, *Janis: Her Life and Music* (Simon & Schuster, 2019)

Joplin, Laura, *Love, Janis* (HarperCollins Publishers Ltd, 1992)

Online

janisjoplin.com (official site)   janisjoplin.net (unofficial)

Biographies

Simon Braund (Author)

Simon Braund is a British music writer. He has been a contributing editor to *Empire*, and his work has appeared in The *Sunday Times,* the *Evening Standard*, the *Financial Times*, *Time Out*, the *Observer, Q* and *Mojo*. He is the co-author of *The Greatest Movies You'll Never See: Unseen Masterpieces by the World's Greatest Directors*, and author of *Orson Welles Portfolio: Sketches and drawings from the Welles Estate*. He divides his time between Cambridge, England, and Los Angeles.

Joel Selvin (Foreword)

Joel Selvin has covered pop music for the *San Francisco Chronicle* since 1970, and has written over 20 books about pop music. His classic, *Summer of Love*, long considered the definitive account of the 1960s San Francisco rock scene, featured interviews with the surviving members of Big Brother and the Holding Company, among many other Joplin associates. His other books include *Red: My Uncensored Life In Rock* with Sammy Hagar, *Altamont*, *Here Comes The Night* and *Hollywood Eden*. Stephen King called Selvin 'a rock legend'.

Picture Credits

Images © Getty Images: Marjorie Alette/Michael Ochs Archives: 20, 24; atlantic-kid/istock: 21; Bettmann: 86, 89, 93, 103; Blank Archives: 83; Bill Bridges/The Life Images Collection: 25; Frederic J. Brown/AFP: 113; CBS Photo Archive: 73; Ed Caraeff: 49; Tom Copi/Michael Ochs Archives: 1, 9, 105, 122, 123; Dick Darrell/Toronto Star via Getty Images: 74; Jay Dickman/Corbis: 98, 111; John Dominis/The Life Picture Collection: 85; David Fenton: 77; GAB Archive/Redferns: 102; Getty Images: 36; Jeff Hochberg: 12; Larry Hulst/Michael Ochs Archives: 106; Hulton-Deutsch Collection/Corbis: 120; Lambert: 42; Elliott Landy/Redferns: 54, 62, 64, 65, 82, 87; Earl Leaf/Michael Ochs Archives: 79; Walter Leporati: 31; Malcolm Lubliner/Michael Ochs Archives: 17, 46, 52; Robert R. McElroy: 28; Malcolm McNeill/Mirrorpix: 78; Frank Mastropolo/Corbis: 15; Michael Ochs Archives: Back cover, 3, 4, 7, 11, 18, 29, 37, 43, 50, 55, 67, 69, 90, 108, 112, 114, 121, 124; Estate Of Keith Morris/Redferns: 75; Terry O'Neill/Iconic Images: 13; Don Paulsen/Michael Ochs Archives: 70; Ron Pownall/Corbis: 66, 128; NY Daily News Archive: 110; Carl Pierce/The Boston Globe: 101; Tucker Ransom/Archive Photos: 58, 116; Paul Ryan/Michael Ochs Archives: 35; Frank Russo/NY Daily News Archive: 104; Donna Santisi/Redferns: 92; Bob Seidemann/Michael Ochs Archives: 38; Julie Snow/Michael Ochs Archives: 56, 60, 61, 127; Ted Streshinsky/Corbis: 26, 41, 51, 53, 57; Stroud/Express: 14; George Tiedemann/Sports Illustrated: Front cover, 88; Charles Tracy/Conde Nast: 94; Chris Walter/WireImage: 117 **Rex Features/Shutterstock:** AP: 16; Apollo/Peach Tree/Kobal: 95; Crawley/Kobal: 19, 118; Fotos International: 107; Peter Larsen: 44, 47; Brian Moody: 76; Wallace/ANL: 81 **SuperStock:** Album: 8, 23, 199; Marka: 32 **WikiCommons:** Brazilian National Archives: 97. Cover image created by Flame Tree Studio, inspired by the poster for Janis Joplin's gig at University of Michigan in Ann Arbor, March 1969